Betty's Bones

By

Terri Daneshyar

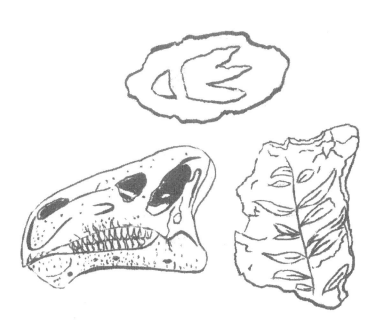

First published in 2019

www.terridaneshyar.com

cover design by Hatice Bayramoglu
Illustrations by sharpesketch.com

ISBN-10: 1796585261
ISBN-13: 9781796585261

Best Wishes

Teri Dansby

Contents

Betty gets inspired

Betty craned her neck to look at the enormous dinosaur skeleton. The huge back legs looked very strong, but the front legs were smaller, and it had a very long tail bone. The deep, round, empty eye sockets held her gaze as she imagined the giant creature roaming around. The information display told her that it was an Iguanodon.

Iguanodons were herbivores, which means they only ate plants. It did have a very long jaw bone, so Betty guessed that it was always chewing.

'Wow!' she said out loud.

A button to her left started a short film of some more dinosaurs, including some of the fiercest ones, which Betty did find a little scary. She imagined riding on the back of a giant Brontosaurus or hiding from a T. Rex. She was completely engrossed in the film when something touched her shoulder.

'Aaaah!' she screamed. 'Dad, don't do that.'

'Sorry, Betty. It's time to leave. The

museum is closing.'

With a sigh, Betty followed Dad towards the exit.

'This place is really interesting, I wish we'd come here before. It's much better than drama club.'

'I thought you liked drama club?'

'I enjoy bits of it, like setting up the stage and stuff, but I'm not really an actor. I only asked to go because Jenny does and she's my best friend, so I thought it would be fun. This is much better.'

Dad smiled and squeezed her hand.

'Well, we will come back next week if you enjoyed it that much.'

'Yes please! Dad, how did they get that

dinosaur in there? And Dad, where did it come from?'

'An archaeologist would have found it in the ground,' said Dad.

'An arky what?' asked Betty.

'An archaeologist. Their job is to find old things buried in the ground and work out what they are. Their discoveries then usually get put on display in a museum. Most of the things in here have been found by archaeologists, although some are found by people just digging in gardens and fields.'

'Could I be an ark … an ark …?'

'Archaeologist,' smiled Dad.

'Yes, one of them.'

'Of course! You could start by digging in our garden – you never know what you might find.'

'No, I mean can I be an arch-ae-o-logist when I'm a grown up?' said Betty.

'I don't see why not. You would have to do a lot of studying and go to university, but if that's what you really want, then you should do it. For now though, start in the garden, maybe right at the bottom where it joins on to the fields.'

*****

All the way home Betty thought about the treasures she would dig up. *I might make a really important discovery*, she thought, and she imagined herself appearing on television telling everyone about it.

'But what I really want … is to find a dinosaur.'

Betty starts to dig

Over the weekend Betty got more and more excited.

'I am going to dig and dig and uncover the massivist dinosaur that's ever been found. It will be huger than this house!' she told Mum. 'And then I will be the most famous arky… arky whatsit in the whole world.'

'That will be brilliant my darling, but do you think you could stop jumping up and down on the sofa? I don't think the springs can take it.'

But Betty was in full flow and continued bouncing and bombarding Mum with how brilliant it was all going to be.

'And when I've found that one, I shall go all over the world to find more. You wait and see.'

She jumped off the sofa and ran upstairs. Ten minutes later she re-emerged wearing her denim dungarees – the kind with lots of pockets – and a purple t-shirt.

'Mum, do you think you could get me some tools so that I can start digging in the garden like Dad said? Please?'

'I shall have my own Indiana Jones,' said Mum, pleased that Betty had calmed down a little. 'What does an archaeologist need?'

Betty had a list of things that she had looked up on the internet and she excitedly gabbled out the items:

'A pencil,

a notebook,

some parcel labels with string,

a toothbrush for cleaning finds,

a box to keep them in,

a triangular-shaped trowel for the careful bits,

a round-edged one for most of the digging!

Please.'

'Slow down, I know you're excited. Ok, my lovely, if you really want to do this, we had better go shopping. Let me finish marking this homework for my class and then we can go to the garden centre. Why don't you get your wellies out of the cupboard and make sure they still fit? Your feet have probably grown since the winter and you might need them even if we are coming into the Spring.'

Mum pinned her hair up in a bun, wrapped her stripy shawl around her shoulders and rushed through the last few Year-Five history projects she had on the table so that she could take Betty shopping.

A couple of hours later Betty was digging

using her round-edged trowel. She also had a triangular one, which they had to get from the DIY shop. It was called a pointing trowel and Betty had to agree, it was very pointy.

Mum and Dad pottered about the garden in case Betty needed them, but she was totally absorbed in her work. In the end they went back indoors for a cup of tea and left Betty to it.

Betty dug and dug and dug. She soon had a large hole in front of her and a large heap of soil behind. Everything she found was examined carefully and written in her notebook:

Earthworms are very wriggly. Found six.

Large stones are hard to get out of the ground.
Found four.
Green glass, shiny but sharp.

Her tummy rumbled. *Five more minutes*, she thought, and began a new hole. There was something white sticking out of the soil. Swapping to her pointy trowel, she began scraping away the dirt to reveal a long thin bone.

'A dinosaur!' she shrieked, jumping up and down with delight.

Carefully picking up her find, she ran down the garden shouting, 'Mum, Dad! I think I've found a dinosaur!'

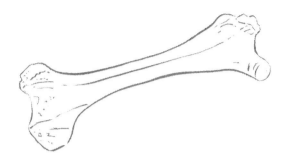

Betty gets a shock

'Well done darling!' said Mum.

'Can I take it to the museum, please Dad? Will they put it on display?'

'They will do tests on it to see what animal it is and how old it is before they display it,' said Dad. 'Clean it, put it in your box and we'll take it after school tomorrow.'

Betty was so excited that night she could hardly sleep.

The next day after school Betty and Dad went to the museum.

'Good afternoon Janice,' said Dad, reading the name badge on the lady at the entrance. 'Could we see the curator please?'

'I have something to show him,' said Betty, proudly holding up the box.

'How wonderful! I'll ring his office for you,' smiled Janice. She picked up her phone.

'Curator, I have a young child here with a find for you. Can you come out to see her?'

Betty didn't hear the reply, just a very

gruff voice on the line. Janice went slightly red but kept smiling at Betty as she was listening.

'If you take a seat, he will … might come out.'

Betty and Dad sat down and waited … and waited … and waited. Time dragged. Dad checked his phone and answered a few emails. Betty fiddled with her hair, tucking it behind her ear nervously. The man that Janice had spoken to didn't sound very friendly. *What if he didn't like her find? What if it wasn't a dinosaur? What if he shouted at her?* All these questions only made her more nervous. Her tummy didn't feel right and what she really wanted at that moment was to go home. She was just about to ask Dad if they could leave when she saw a door open and a rather cross-looking, chubby man stepped through.

'Curator, this is the young lady I rang you about,' said Janice, waving Betty over.

'Another child. Haven't I had to deal with enough of them today. That school group this morning was a total nuisance, touching the displays. And their incessant questions. What happened to children being seen and not heard? And don't tell me it's good for the museum. What's good for the museum are adults who look but don't touch.'

He sighed heavily and snatched Betty's

box from her.

'Another time waster. Let me see, then.'

'I've found a dinosaur bone,' said Betty nervously.

'Humph,' snorted the curator. 'This! This is nothing more than an ordinary cat bone. I suggest you go away and do some reading before wasting my time. How old are you? Seven?'

'I'm eight,' answered Betty, trying not to cry.

'Eight! And you can't tell a cat bone from a dinosaur bone? Please leave. We have to lock up.'

'Just a minute,' said Dad. 'You can't speak to my daughter like that.'

The curator folded his arms, glaring straight at Dad.

'I can, and you should know better than to encourage your child to waste my time.'

He pushed Betty and Dad out of the door and slammed it shut.

'What a rude and horrible man. Are you okay sweetheart? I'm sorry, I should have helped you check out the bone before we brought it.'

Betty was crestfallen. She picked up the bone and shoved it into the first bin they passed, along with her carefully handwritten label. 'Stupid, stupid, stupid,' she said, but underneath her disappointment, a spark of determination took hold as an idea formed in her mind.

'Can we go to the library please, Dad?'

Betty does some research

The library opened late on Thursdays so Betty and Dad still had plenty of time. This was one of Betty's favourite places, full of rows and rows of wonderful stories waiting to be shared. Some of her friends only picked the new books, but if Betty found a book that was a bit worn, she knew it was a sign that lots of people had enjoyed it, so it must be a good read. And Betty loved to read. Sometimes Grandad joked that she was born with a book in her hand, which Betty thought was really funny.

The librarian, whose name was Susan, was at the front desk putting labels in new books.

'Please may I have some books on dinosaur bones?' asked Betty politely. 'I'm going to dig one up and be a famous archaeologist.'

'I think you mean a palaeontologist,' said Susan kindly.

'A pale what?' asked Betty.

'A palaeontologist. They study fossilised animal bones, whereas archaeologists study human artefacts like pottery and jewellery,' said Susan.

'In that case I'm definitely going to be a paleonton, a paletongist … a dinosaur finder,' stated Betty.

Susan smiled. 'Follow me.'

She led them to a whole section of books just on dinosaurs. There were loads! The dinosaur section took up an entire corner. Some of the books were so big and heavy that Dad had to lift them down for her. Betty looked at the ones with brightly coloured covers first, and then later realised that the older ones with plain brown covers had really good sketches inside.

'I never knew there were so many. This is amazing,' smiled Dad.

Betty and Dad were so busy reading that they didn't notice the time until Dad's phone rang loudly. It was Mum.

'We are in the library,' whispered Dad.

He assured Mum that they were ok, then told Betty to choose the books she wanted to borrow.

It was difficult to decide because some books had brilliant pictures but lots of words she didn't understand, and some were too simple. Finally, with help from Susan, Betty had books that were full of information and were just right for her age.

'There are also some excellent websites

to check out. The Natural History Museum is particularly good.'

'Thank you,' said Betty. 'You have been really helpful.'

'All part of the service,' said Susan.

*****

For the next few weeks Betty spent every spare moment learning about dinosaurs and their bones. The names; Stegosaurus, Supersaurus, Triceratops. The sizes and shapes of them. What they ate. Where they were found. She also learnt that Pterosaurs, the flying creatures like Pterodactyl, were not actually dinosaurs, but reptiles. There was so much to find out. Together with her mum and dad, Betty watched lots of TV programmes with the famous naturalist Sir Daniel Attlebury. Some of his shows had very realistic dinosaurs. Betty was fascinated and more determined than ever to prove to the curator that she could identify dinosaur bones when she found them.

'When I find a dinosaur, I'm going to be on telly,' said Betty. 'I'll show that mean old curator.'

Betty digs again

Betty spent six weeks in her bedroom with her books. When her friend Jenny came around to see her, they played a game where Jenny showed Betty a picture of a dinosaur and Betty had to identify it and say three facts about it. It was fun; Jenny liked being the teacher, and Betty liked showing off her new knowledge. Betty even managed to persuade Dad to take her back to the museum again to study the dinosaur bones there. They made very sure to avoid the curator, who seemed to spend most of his time shut in his office, and only spoke to Janice. She was always extremely kind and helpful to Betty.

Once she was certain that she knew what she was looking for, Betty emerged from her room, trowels in hand, and announced that she was going to dig again. She found a spot where the garden joined up to the farmer's field and began. She felt far more confident that this time she would be successful.

For the next few days Betty dug and dug

and dug. Once again, she only managed to find earthworms and stones and a centipede, all of which were carefully recorded in her notebook. On the third day she began to uncover a small white object. Her heart beat quickened as she prised it out of the ground very carefully, then rushed upstairs to look it up. Firstly, she checked on the internet that it wasn't from a cat. *I'm not making that mistake again*, she thought. After that she looked in the encyclopaedia of dinosaurs she had borrowed from the library. It took quite a long time checking what she had found against all the pictures, but then in the middle of the book she got a match. 'Yes!'

she shouted, 'Yes, yes, yes.' To be doubly sure she had correctly identified the bone, she looked it up on her computer as well. Then snatching it up she ran downstairs yelling,

'Mum, Dad, I'm sure this is an Iguanodon's tooth. Can I take it to the museum? I know the curator will be pleased with this.'

'I'm not sure. He was extremely rude last time.'

'I know, but I've learnt loads since then. Please Dad, please!'

'I really don't think it is a good idea. We don't want to get the door slammed on us again.'

'I know Dad, but I want to show him that I can tell a dinosaur from a cat bone. Pleeeease.'

Reluctantly, Dad agreed. Betty filled out a specimen label like a proper palaeontologist, saying where and when it was found, how deep, and of course writing her name. A short car ride later, Dad and a slightly nervous Betty were back at the museum.

'Hello,' said Janice smiling at Betty. 'Have you come to visit the dinosaurs again?'

'No, I'm bringing a piece of a real dinosaur,' said Betty, and she showed Janice the tooth.

'That's brilliant Betty! You've done very well to find that. And you have identified it!'

'Yes, it's from an Iguanodon like the one you have here,' replied Betty proudly.

'I'm sure the curator will be interested in that,' said Janice.

She dialled the curator's number. He was sat at his desk tucking into a large pork pie and he wasn't happy about being interrupted. They heard his gruff voice complaining about being disturbed, as before. However, fifteen minutes later, he emerged from his office brushing crumbs off his rather large belly and attempting to straighten his very messy tie.

'You again. What is it this time? A dead rabbit?'

'Excuse me!' said Dad.

'Actually, it's an Iguanodon's tooth,' said Betty, showing him her specimen, and trying not to giggle at the blob of meat jelly on the end of his nose.

The curator looked in the box.

'So it is.'

'You can have it for your museum,' offered Betty.

'No thank you. I have hundreds. Please don't bother me again.'

He turned and went back down the stairs to his office.

The smile left Betty's face. She gazed

down at the tooth and thought about throwing it away. She was so disappointed.

'I was sure he would be pleased.'

'I don't think that man would be pleased if you walked in with a complete Tyrannosaurus Rex,' said Dad, putting his arm around Betty and giving her a big hug.

'I think your tooth is splendid, and you're very clever to have found it,' said Janice. 'There are not many children who would be able to identify it like you did.'

This made Betty feel much better.

'Thank you,' said Betty. 'It's just, well, I felt so silly when the first thing I brought in was a cat bone, and I've learnt so much about fossils. I want the curator to know that I am serious about bones.'

'You keep on hunting. I am always glad to see what you find. The museum could do with more people as enthusiastic as you,' said Janice. 'I will talk to him and see what I can do.'

'Good luck with that,' said Dad, taking Betty's hand.

'Come on, we'll go and get our own display case and you can put your tooth in our front room.'

'Really Dad? That would be brilliant. Do you think Mum will mind?'

'I think Mum will be just as proud as I am.'

Janice smiled as she watched Betty and

Dad set off, hand in hand, to the shops.

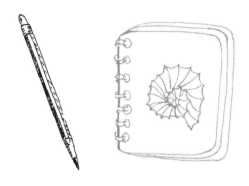

Betty joins a club

Dad put Betty's Iguanodon tooth in a glass case on the front windowsill with a detailed specimen label.

'I've told all my workmates about my clever daughter and her dinosaur find,' said Dad. This made Betty feel proud of herself.

Jenny came to see it too, and told

everyone at school about it. Betty's teacher was so impressed she asked if Betty could bring it in to show the class, which really cheered her up and spurred her on to find more things.

Every weekend Betty would go out digging, enjoying the mild Spring weather. Soon she had three Iguanodon teeth and an ammonite, a spiral shaped fossil, all proudly displayed in cases on the windowsill.

'This is becoming quite a collection,' said Mum.

Betty was very pleased with her discoveries. Her teacher's enthusiasm for the growing collection meant she wanted to find more, and she was still determined to impress the curator.

'There's a palaeontology club in the next village. Why don't we see if you can join?' said Dad.

'Yes please! That would be great,' said Betty. 'Then I can talk to other fossil hunters and see what they have found. Maybe they will tell me the best places to go digging.'

*****

On Wednesday, Betty and Dad went along to join the club. Usually you had to be ten to join, but after Dad explained about Betty's discoveries and how keen she was,

Bill, the chairman in charge of the club, agreed to let her join as long as Mum or Dad came with her each time. She was given a blue badge that said *Junior Palaeontologist*, a leaflet about the club, and a notebook with an ammonite on the cover.

The group was very interesting. At first the older children were unhappy about having such a young member, but once they talked to her and realised how much she knew, they were very encouraging.

One of the members showed a film about a complete dinosaur skeleton he had found on the beach on the Isle of Wight. It was very exciting. Betty made notes all the way through the film, particularly about how many dinosaurs had been discovered on the island. *I'm going to suggest we go there for our holiday,* she thought. *I think it's quite close.*

After that Bill asked members to sign up if they wanted to go on a dig on Saturday. Betty was the first to put her name down.

'Excellent, young lady. Make sure you and your dad are here at the Village Hall, nine o'clock, sharp,' said Bill.

'We will be,' said Dad. They grabbed their coats and headed for the door, joining the other club members who were making their way home.

Betty's day out

Although it was only three sleeps away, it seemed to Betty that Saturday would never arrive. But it did eventually come, and Betty and her Dad were at the Village Hall at nine o'clock.

'Today we are going just along the coast to Ulworth Cove. Let's hope we have a successful day,' said Bill.

Everyone climbed into the minibus and they set off the short distance to Ulworth Cove.

'Do you think we will find dinosaur bones?' Betty asked Bill.

'Well, this is the Jurassic coast, so there is every chance.'

Betty was a bit worried by this reply because she had been allowed to watch a film called *Jurassic Park* when she was at Grandad's. While she liked dinosaur bones, she wasn't sure if she wanted to meet a real, live dinosaur. She tucked her hair behind her ears and held Dad's hand very tightly all the way there.

It wasn't long before they arrived, and

everyone got off and grabbed their bags from the back.

Betty didn't move.

'Come on Betty! I thought you would be the first one off the bus,' said Dad.

Betty just sat very still. She was feeling a little bit sick.

'What's wrong?' asked Dad.

'Will there be a Tyrannosaurus Rex out there? They eat people, you know.'

'No Betty, of course there won't. They are all extinct - they've all died out.'

'But Bill said we are going to Jurassic Park.'

'Oh, Betty you goose,' laughed Dad. 'He said Jurassic coast. It's what this part of

England is called. Not Jurassic Park - that is just a made-up film, and I shall be having words with Grandad. The only dinosaurs here are dead ones buried in the ground.'

Betty fiddled with her hair. 'Are you sure?'

'Quite sure, Betty. Now come on - let's go and dig.'

'Right,' said Betty taking a deep breath. 'I'm ready.'

They got off the bus and went to join the others.

'Everything okay?' asked Bill.

'Yes thank you, just a little mix up. We are ready to go now,' smiled Dad, squeezing Betty's hand.

'Excellent. Well, happy digging!'

Betty and Dad wandered off to find a good spot. They settled on a place at the base of the cliff, got out their trowels and began to dig. Dad had no idea what he was looking for, but Betty was keeping a close eye on things.

'Look, look Dad, I've found something.'

Very carefully, using her pointy trowel and toothbrush, Betty began to clear away the sand and rock to reveal a stone with a pattern on it.

'Bill, Bill,' shouted Betty. 'I've found something.'

Bill came over to see what she had uncovered.

As Betty cleared the sand, she revealed a beautiful spiral shaped object.

'An ammonite,' said Betty.

'Yes, and that's a particularly good one. It must be over five centimetres. Well done, well done young lady.'

'Thank you, Bill. Shall I put it in my specimen box?'

'Yes, make sure to label it.'

'I will,' said Betty, getting out her notebook to draw what she had found.

Although Betty didn't find anything else, she had a wonderful day digging and looking at other finds. Between them the group found six ammonites, a brittle star and a prehistoric fish skeleton.

When they got back to the Village Hall, all the discoveries made by the club members were re-labelled, photographed, and then sent off to Lyme Regis Museum. The people there kept a record of all the fossils that were found locally. This was called cataloguing and it was very important because it allowed palaeontologists to understand more about the types of dinosaurs that had lived in the area.

Betty was very pleased with her find, but a little disappointed that she couldn't take it home.

'Don't worry,' said Dad. 'I'm sure you will find more things you'll be able to keep.'

Betty nodded. She had kept most of her other finds and she wanted to keep adding to her collection. When they got home, she rushed into the house to tell Mum all about their day.

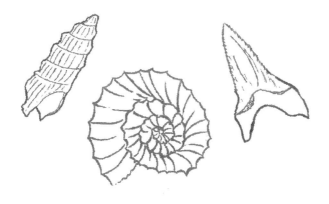

Betty's busy summer

All through the summer Betty continued going out with the palaeontologist's club and helping them find new fossils for the Lyme Regis Museum. She also carried on her own excavations. Whenever she found something, she would take it along to her museum and show it to Janice at the front desk, who was always interested. Each time

Janice would ring the curator to come and check the find, but each time he was as rude and dismissive as ever.

'Really child, this is becoming very tiresome. I simply don't need to look at yet another ammonite or fossilised fish or Plesiosaur bone. Unless you are going to bring me something unusual, stop bothering me.'

He turned to Janice. 'If I have to deal with any more children, you will be finding yourself another job. I had another school party in today. That's the third one this month!'

He returned to his office, slamming the door behind him.

'I see his manners haven't improved,' said Dad. 'How do you manage to work for him?'

Janice sighed, 'I love this museum and meeting all the people who come in. I studied archaeology at university, so working with the exhibits is perfect for me. Fortunately, he stays in his office most of the time.'

'It is a very interesting place,' said Betty. 'I'm always telling my friends to come here. Some of the children in my class call me a nerd, but I don't care. My friends don't, they like to hear about the fossils and my teacher too. I don't know why you have to be unkind to someone just because they like different things to you. I don't call them names for preferring computer games.'

'Unfortunately, Betty, that's the way some people are,' said Janice.

'Well I think we should just be nicer to each other.' said Betty.

'I agree,' said Dad looking towards the curator's office.

'Definitely,' smiled Janice.

The next day Betty and Dad set off to the coast for a day of digging.

'I haven't had this much fun for years,' said Dad. 'I really enjoy our days out together.'

'Me too,' said Betty. 'I did ask Mum if

she wanted to come as well, but she said that she and I do lots of things together, and it's great for us to have time to ourselves.'

'Oh, did she?' smiled Dad.

'Yes, she said it was nice to have some peace and quiet to read her books.'

'Marvellous,' grinned Dad. 'Everyone is happy.'

He held Betty's hand and they went for a good long walk along the sand dunes looking for a place to dig.

'Well, this looks like an excellent spot. Shall we start here?' asked Dad, picking a place high up the beach at the base of the cliffs. 'I remember you found that large ammonite near the cliffs, so maybe we'll get lucky today.'

They got out their trowels and started clearing the sand. Underneath, the earth was more gravelly.

'If we dig a bit deeper, we might find something,' said Betty. 'I remember the man who found the skeleton on the Isle of Wight said he went down about fifteen centimetres.'

At first, they didn't find anything remarkable; just one small ammonite. Dad clapped his hands.

'This is great, we can add this one to your display at home!'

Betty wasn't listening. She pawed at the

ground like an excited dog, then grabbed her brush and carefully, heart pounding, began to brush away more of the earth.

'I think I've found something! Dad! Dad look, there are some teeth.'

Slowly, slowly, Betty and Dad began to uncover the find. By the time they had cleared away the sand and soil, they had uncovered what looked like a large jawbone, complete with teeth. The whole thing was nearly a metre long. It was difficult to tell who was more thrilled, Betty or Dad.

'This is amazing, Betty. What do you think it is? A lizard, one like a Plesiosaur?'

'I'm not sure. If we get it home, I can

look it up on my computer and in my books.'

Very carefully, Betty and Dad lifted the bone out of the ground and wrapped it in the picnic rug they had brought with them. They took it back home to show Mum, who was delighted.

'That is amazing. It's huge. How did you manage to get it back to the car? Wow!'

Betty washed it very carefully and they put it on the big kitchen table. She brought her books downstairs, then with Dad's help, she managed to work out that it was a herbivore of some kind, due to the blunt shape of the teeth.

'This will finally make the curator take

notice,' smiled Betty. 'If only because of its size.'

The next morning Betty, Mum and Dad set off to the museum, with Betty's find carefully labelled and boxed.

Janice looked in the box and her eyes lit up. 'Wow, Betty, that is impressive. I'll call the curator right away!'

The curator was in a particularly bad mood that day. He had just received a letter from the museum's director, saying that if the attendance figures didn't go up the museum would have to close. Janice had made lots of suggestions of how to help, but as they all involved more local schools, he had ignored them.

'If I didn't have to keep dealing with that child, I would be able to get more adults in here. Adults don't waste my time or touch things,' he shouted down the phone to Janice. 'Tell her to go away.'

'I'm afraid the curator is too busy to see you today, but if you would like to leave your find here, I will make sure that someone looks at it.'

Mum and Dad weren't sure, but Betty was determined to show it to the curator. Putting on her most serious face she said,

'I'll leave it until tomorrow, but then I'm going to take it to Lyme Regis because I know that they will be interested.'

'Leave it with me,' said Janice.

Janice makes a call

After they had gone, Janice had a good long look in the box. Then she went into her tiny office, where she had covered the walls in postcards from around the world. Some were places she had been, but most were places that she wanted to visit. Checking for the right number, she called the palaeontology department of the

Natural History Museum in London.

By early afternoon, a tall young woman with purple streaks in her brown hair and wearing a bright red neck scarf arrived at the museum.

'I'm looking for Janice,' she said in a very business-like manner as she came to the front desk.

'That's me,' said Janice.

'I believe you have something for me?' said the lady in the neck scarf.

'Oh yes,' said Janice excitedly, and showed her into the tiny office where she had safely stowed Betty's box. It only took a moment for the visitor to know that this was a rather special bone.

'This is very interesting, very interesting indeed. Who found it?'

'A young lady called Betty. She is always bringing things, but the curator says he doesn't need them,' said Janice.

'Can you get her here, please? I'd like to talk to her.'

Janice rang the number Dad had left with her. There was a brief conversation. Fifteen minutes later Betty and her Dad were in the museum, just as the curator was making his rounds. He looked at Betty.

'You again! I thought I told you not to bother me.'

'We haven't come to see you,' said Betty 'We've come to see Professor Cooper.'

'Never heard of him.'

'Her, actually,' said a voice from behind him.

The curator turned around to see the lady in the red scarf.

'You must be Betty,' she said, looking straight at the little girl. 'I'm so pleased to meet you. I wonder if you and your father would like to come back to London with me to analyse your find?'

'What find?' spluttered the curator. 'Not another one of her brittle star nonsense?'

'I'm afraid, as you weren't interested you will just have to wait and see, won't you?' answered Professor Cooper.

'It's my museum. If it's of interest I

should check it out,' burbled the curator.

'You had your chance,' said Professor Cooper, leading Betty and Dad out to her car, followed by Janice carrying the box. With the bone safely onboard Professor Cooper drove them home to tell Mum what was happening and to pack an overnight bag.

'I'm sorry we can't fit you in the car as well,' said Professor Cooper to Mum.

'That's okay,' said Mum. 'The fossil hunting is something Betty and her Dad like to do together.' Secretly though, she was a little disappointed not to be going with them this time.

*****

When the professor's car was out of sight, Janice went slowly back inside the museum, hoping the curator had returned to his office. Unfortunately, he was standing waiting for her, arms folded, with a thunderous look on his face.

'How dare you bring that woman into my museum, overriding my authority? Consider this a warning. Any more antics like that, and you will be looking for a new job!'

'Don't you want to know what Betty found?' asked Janice.

'It won't be anything important. People make too much fuss over children if you ask me. Now can we lock up? It's early closing day.'

He returned to his office, leaving Janice to close the museum.

Betty goes to London

Professor Cooper drove Betty and Dad to London. All the way there, she was asking Betty questions about where she found the bone. How deep it was buried? What was the soil like? Was there anything else in the ground? Betty answered the best she could.

'What do you think it is, Professor?' asked Betty hopefully.

'I'm not sure yet Betty. Our tests will tell us a lot more. Do you mind if I ask what made you want to find fossils?'

Betty thought for a moment.

'It was the dinosaur in our local museum that started it. I couldn't believe how big it was! And then our librarian was really helpful, showing me which books to read. She even told me about your Natural History Museum website. Mum and Dad helped too. We always watch those programmes with Sir Daniel Attlebury, where they make the dinosaurs look so real. Have you seen them?'

'Yes, I have. In fact, I helped them to make those programmes.'

'Wow, that's amazing! They are my favourite thing to watch.'

'I'm so glad you like them,' Professor Cooper smiled.

When they arrived at the museum, Professor Cooper took them up to her department. They went through a door marked '*Staff Only*' which Betty found quite exciting, knowing that most people weren't allowed in there. Behind the doors were rows and rows of glass cases with all sorts of bones in. There were carefully labelled drawers which Professor Cooper said contained even smaller bones. At the end of the corridor they entered a room that looked like a laboratory. It had jars and test tubes and strange looking machines. Professor Cooper put on a white coat like a hospital doctor's and gave one to Dad to wear too.

'I'm sorry Betty we don't have one in your size.'

'That's okay,' said Betty disappointedly.

Professor Cooper saw her face.

'Wait here a moment. Please don't touch anything.' She disappeared through another door and came back a few minutes later with a small white coat.

'Here try this. It's from the school room.'

Betty put it on. It was a little bit big but she didn't mind.

'I feel like a proper scientist,' she said.

'Now Betty, I need you to put the bone onto this tray please,' said Professor Cooper, indicating a large, rectangular piece of glass with slightly raised sides.

Very carefully, Betty and Dad placed the bone onto the tray.

'I'm going to put it into this machine. It is called a CT scanner, and it's going to take pictures all the way through the bone.'

'Like an X-ray?' said Betty.

'Yes, like an X-ray, only much more detailed,' said Professor Cooper.

'I had an X-ray when I fell off my bike. They looked at the bones in my arm. They weren't broken, but it was very interesting.'

Professor Cooper smiled at Betty.

'This will be interesting too, Betty. Come and look.'

She took Betty into the next room where they were able to look at the pictures of the bone that the scanner was taking.

'This machine will tell us what this creature ate, how old the bone is, and what species.'

'That's amazing. It's a lot quicker than looking in my books,' said Betty.

The scanner took pictures, and the computer in the office flashed up lots of images, trying to match the bone to all the dinosaur information it had. When the scan was finished, Professor Cooper turned to

Betty with a big smile on her face.

'Betty, this is absolutely wonderful. We haven't seen anything like this before.'

'What does that mean?' asked Dad.

'It means that young Betty here has discovered a brand-new species of dinosaur. There is nothing in our database to match it. Would you like to name it, Betty?'

'Oh, yes please!' She thought about it. 'Could I call it a Betisaurus?'

'You can indeed.'

The professor had to complete some forms and write up a report. While she was doing all this, she got someone to show Betty and her Dad around the dinosaur exhibit in the museum, even though it was closing time. The mechanical dinosaurs were thrilling, although Betty did hold Dad's hand extra tightly when the T-rex started to roar. There were so many different skeletons and loads of interactive screens.

'Dad, look at this,' said Betty, pointing to a Stegosaurus. 'And this, oh my gosh and this!'

Betty ran from exhibit to exhibit, starting the information loops and then moving on to the next thing before the voice had chance to get going. It was all too exciting. Dad couldn't keep up with her enthusiasm, especially as he was trying to read all the information himself.

When the Professor was finished, Betty and Dad went back to her office.

'Well Betty, your Betisaurus is a herbivore, a plant eating dinosaur. It is a therapod, a small herbivore that walked on two legs. A new species. This is very, very exciting news. There is one more thing you have to do. I need you to sign this paper, which details where you found it and the results of the CT scan, and then the Betisaurus will be an official dinosaur.'

Professor Cooper called the museum photographer to take pictures of Betty and her bone. Then another man came and asked her lots of questions for an article to go on the museum's website.

'Thank you. You are so much nicer than that awful curator at our local museum,' said Dad. 'He is such a rude man.'

'Well we are not going to encourage more people into our museums with his attitude, are we?' said Professor Cooper.

She arranged for Dad and Betty to stay in a hotel for the night. They called Mum, who was waiting at home for news. They told her everything that had happened. Betty talked so fast Mum had trouble keeping up, but she was really, really pleased for her little girl.

The next morning, Betty and Dad were able to explore the Natural History

Museum. It was such an interesting place. There was so much to see and do! There were meteorites, birds, and loads of information about Charles Darwin, the Victorian scientist. Betty also found a reptile on display which was named after Sir Daniel. Of course, they went back to the dinosaur section, and even though the life-sized moving dinosaurs were just a little bit scary, that was definitely Betty's favourite part of the museum. The day passed very quickly, and Betty and Dad were rather disappointed when Professor Cooper said it was time to drive them back home.

'What will happen to my dinosaur?'

asked Betty.

'We would like to keep it at the Natural History Museum, if that's okay with you Betty?'

Betty tucked her hair behind her ears and went quiet.

Professor Cooper frowned. 'I thought you would be pleased? I promise we will take great care of it.'

'I know that,' replied Betty. 'It's just that I wanted to show the curator that I can actually find a proper dinosaur. He's been so horrible and he thinks I'm a time-waster. And Janice has been so nice to me and I know that he is rude to her too. If he knew how important my find is, he might be kinder to her.'

'Leave it to me, Betty,' said Professor Cooper. 'I know just what to do.'

Betty makes the News

When Betty and Dad got back home, Betty told Mum even more about the Natural History Museum and the tests they did on her dinosaur bone. Dad showed Mum the photographs he had taken on his phone.

'It was such an amazing place! Please can we go there again?' asked Betty.

'Of course we can, Betty. Mum has to go

and see your dinosaur when it's on display,' said Dad. 'We would have taken her the first time if there had been room in the car, but your bone took up too much space!'

'I've definitely got to go,' said Mum. 'We could go for a weekend and really take our time in the museum. Would you like that Betty?'

'Definitely. Thanks Mum.'

Later that week, Betty had a phone call from the local newspaper. They wanted to interview her about her find. Mum and Dad said that it was okay, so a reporter from *The Lyme Regis Echo* came to the house. Her name was Rebecca. She asked Betty lots of questions about where she found the bone. How long had she been interested in palaeontology? What was the name of the palaeontology club she was in? How helpful the local museum had been?

'Janice, the curator's assistant, was very helpful. She called Professor Cooper,' said Betty.

'What about the curator? I'm sure he would have been very interested in your find?' said Rebecca.

'Oh no, he didn't even look at it. He just told me to go away and stop bothering him.'

'Really?' replied Rebecca. 'That is very interesting. Did you often bother him?'

'Well, I always took my finds in to show

him first, before I sent them off to Lyme Regis.'

'He was always extremely rude to her,' said Dad, 'But she insisted on going to show him.'

'So, if it wasn't for Janice recognising you had found something special, Professor Cooper wouldn't have got involved?'

'That's right, Rebecca. She knew that Betty had found something important,' said Mum.

'Thank you,' said Rebecca. 'I think I've got enough information for my piece. If we could just take a couple of pictures? My photographer is waiting in the car.'

Betty happily smiled for the camera.

'I'll send you a copy of the article when I've written it,' she said. 'It should be in the weekend edition.'

'Thank you,' said Betty.

When the article appeared in the local paper, the headline read;

'*Dinosaur Discovery Dismissed.*'

It told the story of Betty being ignored by her local museum curator, how The Natural History Museum got involved, and how Betty had discovered a brand-new dinosaur. It was very exciting, but Betty was a little worried that it would make the curator angry.

Later that day, Betty had another phone call. This time it was Professor Cooper.

'Hello Betty. I hope you don't mind, but I'm coming to see you tomorrow, and I'll be bringing your fossil with me.'

'That's brilliant, I'd like to see it again.'

'Yes, I'm sure you would. Could I have a word with your Mum please?'

Betty handed the phone to Mum. She couldn't hear what the professor was saying, but Mum kept nodding and smiling and saying *fine* and *super*.

Mum wouldn't tell Betty what the professor had told her, she just kept saying it was a surprise.

'You'll find out in the morning, Betty.'

'Will I like it? Is it a trip to the Natural History Museum?'

'I'm not telling you, but I think that you will be very happy,' said Mum. 'Very happy indeed.'

Betty's big day

The next morning, Mum told Betty to wear the clothes that she wore on her last dig and to bring her trowels and notebook with her.

'Are we going on a dig then?' asked Betty.

'No, we are all going to the local museum.'

Betty was very puzzled. She had never had to take her trowels with her to the museum before.

When they got to the museum there were an awful lot of people there, and lots of vans with strange looking aerials on the top parked outside. Betty started to feel very nervous. Tucking her hair behind her ears, she held Mum's hand very tightly. Then she heard a familiar voice.

'Morning Betty! Don't look so worried. These are television vans. They are here to meet you. You are going to be on the television.'

Betty was very pleased to see Professor Cooper.

'On television!' said Betty. 'Me?'

'Yes. Come with me,' and Professor Cooper took Betty's hand and led her around to the front of the museum where there was even more equipment, and one more surprise.

Standing there ready to interview Betty was Sir Daniel Attlebury, the famous television naturalist.

'Wow, this is amazing! Is he really going to talk to me?'

'Oh yes Betty, you have made a very important discovery and people need to know about it.'

Sir Daniel came over and shook Betty's hand warmly. He told her they were going to make a short film for schools to encourage other children to get interested in palaeontology and part of it was also going to be shown on the local news channel. They moved to the filming area where her dinosaur was there in its case, with some pictures of what the whole creature might have looked like. He asked Betty lots of questions and listened very attentively to her replies. He also included Professor Cooper and Janice.

It was all going extremely well when the doors of the museum burst open, and out came the curator.

'What is going on? Where is my assistant? Get these people away from my museum. How are visitors supposed to get in with all these trucks here?'

Then he saw Betty.

'And what is that annoying child doing here?'

The TV camera turned towards the curator as Sir Daniel Attlebury approached him.

'This lovely young lady has discovered a brand-new species of dinosaur.'

'Impossible! She can't even tell a cat bone when she finds one.'

'Perhaps you would care to take a look at this, then?' offered Sir Daniel, leading the curator to the specimen case and the display behind it.

The curator looked at the jawbone and the pictures and then at Betty, who was standing there beaming.

'She couldn't possibly have found that.'

Just then, Rebecca from *The Lyme Regis Echo* stepped forward.

'Curator, would you like to make a comment for our readers about how you missed the chance to help in this historic discovery?'

'Well… well, yes. You see I get so many children who think they have discovered things and this girl in particular is always badgering me. How was I supposed to know this one was important?'

'You are never interested. I've been

trying to show you how much I have learned for ages. Lyme Regis Museum look at my finds. They have got most of them on display,' said Betty.

'If they want to bother with children, that's up to them. I am far too busy,' said the curator.

'Too busy for a brand-new dinosaur? Surely not…' said Sir Daniel.

'Well, well … her first discovery was a cat bone. How could I possibly take her seriously after that?'

'Perhaps you should have been more encouraging instead of dismissing her,' said Sir Daniel. 'She is clearly a determined young lady. We must inspire visitors into our museums, not push them away.'

'Adult visitors,' said the curator. 'Only adult visitors!' And stormed back indoors.

Sir Daniel turned back to the camera and finished his interview with Betty.

The curator sulked in his office, trying to work out what to say when the museum director heard about today's events.

'Pesky child,' he muttered. 'If it wasn't for her and Janice, with her interfering ways, my job would be so much easier.'

He got up, feeling thoroughly bad tempered and stuck a very large **Do Not Disturb** sign on his office door.

When the television crews had finished, Betty, Dad, Mum, Janice, Professor Cooper and Sir Daniel Attlebury all went off to have a delicious afternoon tea together.

Betty decided that this was the best day of her life. Ever!

Acknowledgements

A big thank you to my fellow StoryVine members, Jenny Heap, Sue Newgas and Rowen Wilde for their continued support and critiquing. Jenny, thank you so much for your hard work on the formatting.

To my editor Ellen Morris for her advice and enthusiasm for this project. To Alex for sharing her story, she really did discover a dinosaur.

To Heidi and Lindsay Lewis and Lottie Johnson for being my first readers. Thank you for your positive response to Betty.

A special thank you to Haticeby for producing a wonderful cover, check her out on facebook at The Art of HB. And to Alan Sharpe at sharpesketch.com for the glorious illustrations.

Thank you to our amazing museums and libraries and the wonderful people who work there. I'm sure none of them are as grumpy as my curator. Make sure to use them.

And finally, a big thank you to you for reading my book and posting a positive review on Amazon or Goodreads (if you have).

If you want to find out more about my books go to terridaneshyar.com.

Printed in Poland
by Amazon Fulfillment
Poland Sp. z o.o., Wrocław